Why Did You Choose to
Get Pregnant?

A Teenagers guide to overcoming the social and emotional implications of teen pregnancy

DR. LATESHIA WOODLEY

authorHOUSE®

AuthorHouse™
1663 Liberty Drive
Bloomington, IN 47403
www.authorhouse.com
Phone: 1-800-839-8640

First published by AuthorHouse 2/21/2011

ISBN: 978-1-4567-3930-0 (e)
ISBN: 978-1-4567-3931-7 (sc)

Library of Congress Control Number: 2011902752

Printed in the United States of America

ACKNOWLEDGEMENTS

I acknowledge God who is the center of my life and without him none of this would be possible.

I acknowledge and humbly thank Mr. William Greene Principal of the Perry Learning Center and Dr. Darian Jones, Principal of Carver Health Science and Research High School. Through their vision and openness to reach out to teen parents paved the way for the birth of this project.

I acknowledge my offspring and surrogate offspring Alex, Alexis, Aliana, Araya for their participation in this journey.

I acknowledge the love of my life Alex for never complaining and always being my support system.

I acknowledge and humbly thank my partners, students, friends and supporters of Dynamic Achievement Solutions, LLC.

FORWARD

Teen Pregnancy is not only a medical issue it is also Mental Health Issue. When a teenager is suspected of being pregnant, the first order of business is to send them to a medical doctor to deal with the medical issues. The social and emotional issues that the teenagers are facing are never taken into consideration. The standard of care does not include a referral to counselor or marriage and family therapist. This is essential to the health of the teen and their unborn child. The standard of care for working with pregnant teens should include a referral to mental health professional to monitor the social and emotional needs of the teen as the ultrasound monitors the growth and development of the baby.

This book serves as a guide to assist teenagers in working through their social and emotional issues as they find themselves in the middle of two worlds colliding. The mission is to ignite, motivate and encourage teen parents to reach their full potential.

TABLE OF CONTENTS

Scene One

Scene Two

Scene Three

Scene One

Why did you Choose to Get Pregnant?

Welcome! Chances are if you have been given this book you are a teen parent or currently pregnant. You probably think that your life is falling apart. You are probably experiencing a flood of emotions which include denial, anger, depression, blaming, acceptance and joy to name a few. All of which is normal as you find yourself at this major life transition.

The objective of this book is to assist you in navigating these emotions and social challenges that you are facing or about to face. We are going to explore every inch of your emotional shipwreck and help you transition from this experience to the accomplishment of all your dreams. Let me warn you that this will not be easy. You must make a firm commitment to do the work and design the life that you want. Know that your life does not end when you become pregnant. You can still accomplish all your goals and dreams. So if you are ready take a deep breath and Lets Get To Work!

Ask Your self this question:
"Why did I choose to get pregnant?"

My Story

At age 15 and about 5 months pregnant, I walked into my high School as though it was a foreign place. Eyes seem to follow me through the hallways as I walked to my homeroom class. After arriving at my homeroom class, I was quickly removed from class and sent to the counselor's office.

In the counselors office I was informed that pregnancy was a disease that would spread like wild fire if I was allowed to walk the halls. Six other girls had caught this disease over the summer as well.

The school came up with a plan to quarantine the seven of us in the home economics room. In the pregnant girls room as we called it there was a refrigerator, stove, bathroom, couch and a bed. Everything we needed. We even had a private entrance through the back of the school.

The second day in the pregnant girls room the question came. Why did you choose to get pregnant?

A flood of emotions came over me and I quickly became defensive and stated that it was a mistake an accident it was not a choice.

The counselor looked me straight in my eyes and said sweetheart getting pregnant is not an accident, it is a choice. If you don't begin to understand that it is a choice and why you made the decision, you will be back here pregnant again next year.

Since that time I have reflected on my decisions to get pregnant and every teen parent workshop I facilitate I ask the question and the response seems universal "It was a mistake or an accident". I believe that the discovery of the answer to this question come through the evaluation of your relationships with the people in your life and the situations and events that were going on prior to your decision to get pregnant. The following are some reflective questions to help guide you in your discovery of your answer to the question why did you choose to get pregnant.

Reflection Questions

Think about the time leading up to your conception. What was going on in your life?

_____

_____

What was your relationship like with your parents?

_____

_____

What was the relationship like with your child's father?

_____

_____

Did you like school? Were you apart of any extra-curricular activities?

_____

_____

Describe your feelings or emotions during this time (ie. anger, depression, joy, love).

_____

_____

Why did you choose to get pregnant?

_____

_____

Teen Parent Responses

Oh yea I can finally answer your question. Why did I get pregnant? I don't have any kind of male like father figure around me. I miss the father daughter love and connection I had with my father. He died five years ago on thanksgiving. After that I would cling to my uncles and hope for the same connection. One of my uncles faded away because of drug usage. And the other to begin to get caught up with intermediate family problems and/ or moved away from me. I clinged to the next thing. another male. This time it was one my age. I felt needy for love from a male, until it got out of control. I went out with the boy and started doing things that I would not normally do because it was new to me or I thought he would leave. Now I have more confidence. If you would not have asked that question I would not have came closer to really knowing who I am. Thank you.

Because I didn't have a father and my mom was busy working to provide for me and my other three sisters and brothers. I was brainwashed and thought I was in love.

I felt unloved and wanted attention. I needed someone to love me and I used sex as a way of feeling loved.

I thought my boyfriend really loved me and this was a way that we would be together forever.

Family problems and relationship problems. I had to fight all my life. I chose to get pregnant to obtain freedom from my situation.

7

I wasn't being cautious of my action. Not thinking of the consequences. Low self-esteem, not thinking enough of myself to practice safe sex.

I chose to get pregnant because I had just had an abortion and felt guilty.

I did not choose to get pregnant, I was raped.

Well I was one of those girls that was not interested in boys yet. I was twelve years old and my aunt's husband started molesting me. It went on for years before I got pregnant. He told me that nobody would want me because I was ugly. I was scared to have a boyfriend or tell anyone what was going on. At age eighteen I got pregnant. I felt very embarrassed and afraid to tell my family who the father was. I prayed that my son would look like me and not like his father. I finally told my mother and she was devastated. My family turned against me and acted as though I came on to him. My aunt thought the same thing. I asked god why me? I feel that my teenage years were ripped away from me. Why was I so unlovable?

My Story

At the time of my conception my family was in a state of division. I grew up in a small town and lived between my grandmother and my aunt's house. My mother was a workaholic living in another state and my father was the town's alcoholic. Two years prior to me getting pregnant I was living with my aunt and her husband began to touch me inappropriately. I shared this information with my grandmother and it destroyed my family. The family members began to take sides. One of the loudest dissenters was my great grandmother. Her comments were stamp permanently into my mind. She told my aunt that I was a fast girl trying to take her husband and she needed to get me out of her house anyway. Prior to this experience I was an honor roll student and involved in many extra-curricular activities at school like cheerleading, beauty pageants, Ms. Homecoming to name a few. I felt alone and unloved. I met my son's father through a friend. He was very smart and popular. He begins to shower me with attention which I so desperately needed at the time. Because of his popularity I felt that I needed to have sex with him to keep his interest. I chose to get pregnant so that I could have some one to love and some one to love me back.

Understanding Your Emotions

In the process of working this book you will have many revelations. You may experience a flood of emotions from decisions that you made or things that others may have said or done to you. You may become overwhelmed with sadness, anger or depression. Stop! Put the book down. If you feel the need to stomp, scream, cry, laugh, or throw something that is unbreakable then do so. Relax, take a nice bath or shower. It is something about the cleansing power of water that enables your to see things a little more clearly. Once you have composed your self let's continue through the process.

Redefining the World around You

From the moment that you find out that you are pregnant, the world around you seems to change. Your family, friends and child's father immediately turn into different people. You begin to question who you are and try to find a way to function within the dysfunction. Your first task is to share the news of your pregnancy with your social circle.

Those of you who have completed this step know that this is one of the most difficult tasks that you will ever encounter in life. It is also a task that will be brandied into the corners of your mind forever. This experience can have a major effect on your emotional and sometimes physical well being. It is very important that you process this experience and deal with the emotional implications that may have resulted.

On the worksheet that follows, you will be asked to evaluate your social circle. Your social circle is the people in your life that you shared the news with about your pregnancy. This may include family, friends, teachers, child's father, and child's father's family. This activity is designed to assist you in becoming conscious of the emotions, thoughts, experiences and beliefs that have may be encountering as a result of revealing your pregnancy.

My Story

As a result of my family problems I moved away from my small town to the Hot Atlanta Georgia with some of my other family members. I did not realize it then but I was very depressed. I went to school daily with not a care about my appearance; which was the very opposite of my personality. I continued to make good grades but I did not form any relationships with any of the staff or students at the new school. I merely existed.

I continued a long distance relationship with my boyfriend back home. The family members that I was living with at the time did not have a phone so I would schedule a time with my boyfriend to call him collect from a pay phone. In one of those prearranged phone calls we decided that I would come to visit him and go the prom. I did go home to visit but we never made it to the prom.

After our intimacy encounter I instantly felt different. I went back to Atlanta and within a few weeks I began having dizzy spells and mourning sickness. The first person I told was my boyfriend. He was amazingly very calm and told me to calm down until we knew for sure. We both agreed that we were not ready to be parents. I was in the 9th grade he was in the 11th grade. I wanted to give the baby up for adoption he wanted me to have an abortion. The thought that he would have a child somewhere out in the world that he did not know was too much for him to handle.

The next person I told was my aunt that I was living with in Atlanta. She was a teen mom and was very sympathetic to my situation. She then told my uncle who went ballistic. He was already struggling to take care of a wife and three kids all under five and had brought me into his home as well. He was not a happy camper. His only question to me was do you have a plan. I said I did not. He said you need to develop a plan quickly and start by calling your mother. My mother who was also a teen mother lost her mind. She flew to Atlanta and took me to the doctor with the firm commitment that this pregnancy problem must go away. I tried to reason with her to allow me to have the baby and give it up for adoption. I begged her not to force me have an abortion. She said that if I decided to have the baby she would never speak to me again. She did not talk to me the entire time I was pregnant.

The moment of truth came when I had to go back to my small town and tell my family members there that I was pregnant. I remember getting in the bed with my grandmother straddling her holding her hands and saying mama I got something to tell you but promise me you are not going to get upset. She said ok. I said I am pregnant and she threw me across the room. As GOD fearing as she was she was also adamant that I was going to get an abortion. She called my mother's three sisters and other two brothers to inform them of my fall from grace. Two of my aunts were very supportive of my adoption plan but one physically assaulted me when I informed her that I did not want to have an abortion. One of my uncles told me that I was failure and a disgrace to the family; I was going to be nothing but a statistic, sperm receptacle and welfare recipient.

My grandmother called a meeting with my boyfriend's family to discuss the matter. His mother begged my grandmother not to force me to have an abortion and offered to allow me to move in with them until the baby was born. His parents agreed to care for the baby until both my boyfriend and I finished college. So the decision was made. My grandmother did not agree to allow me to move in with his family but if they were going to take on the responsibility of my medical care while I was pregnant and the baby after it was born then she would allow me to have the baby and live with her during the pregnancy.

Evaluating Your Social Circle

Think about all the individuals that you shared the news of your pregnancy with. Ask your self the following questions. What was their response? What was their reaction? Complete the circle below with this information. Add circles to include all the people in your social circle.

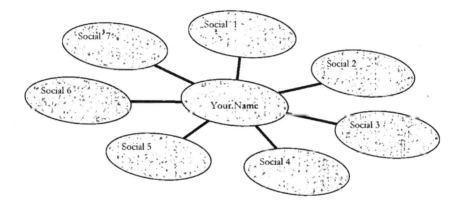

Take some time to reflect on your social circle exercise. Reread your responses and jot down your thoughts into this reflection chart. Begin with your reaction to the news of your pregnancy. You may find it helpful to make a copy of this page before you begin or use scratch paper.

Social Circle Member	Response/Reaction	Effect Socially and Emotionally
(Teen Mom)		

What Does Love Have to Do With This?

You look and the mirror and see your body being stretched beyond what your mind can conceptualize. You sit back and watch as the teenagers around you make plans for their social events as you look at your calendar to make plans for your doctor's appointments. The teenagers around you are out shopping for the latest trends, you are searching for something to fit.

Your mind begins to play a series of negative commercials and you begin to demonstrate in your appearance the woe is me mentality. You began to feel ashamed of your current state. You realize that fairy tale experience you have imagined quickly turns into Nightmare on Elm Street. Nothing and no one is living up to the imagined expectations that you created in your mind. You begin to question the true meaning of love and wonder how you got stuck in this unfamiliar territory.

During this time you may find yourself being very emotional. Crying becomes a normal part of your daily routine. You may find yourself isolating from others as they isolate from you. When you try to force yourself to continue with your daily routine you may feel like you don't belong or fit in. The major topic of conversation is how big your stomach is getting and the ultimate can I touch your stomach. Everyone wants to touch the very thing that you wish that you could hide.

My Story

A couple weeks after the revelation to God and country that I was in fact pregnant, my boyfriend left to attend this pre-college math and science summer program for six weeks. I immediately felt abandoned. I was only 15 and unable to get a job. I expected him to decline the program and work to save some money to prepare for the baby. I was in a state of total confusion. I cried for breakfast, lunch and dinner. I was plagued by advice from my social circle that men were no good. My grandmother's advice was all men will do is fill you up with a house full of children and run off and marry someone else. One of my aunt's advice was never count on a man for anything he will always let you down. My mother words hurt the worst, she said "he is going to be focused on books while you are worried about pampers". Those messages as well as the other messages from my social circle played like negative infomercials in the corner of my mind. I placed myself in total isolation from everyone that summer.

Upon my boyfriend return from the pre-college program, I was in a state of nervous unrest. Instead of getting a job, he immediately began practicing and getting ready for football season. Unfortunately, they were not accepting pregnant cheerleaders that season so I had to sit on the sidelines. Football season came and went and basketball season began. He was having the time of his life as I was getting as big as a house. I constantly told that I looked like I was having twins. I began to think and feel that I was a serious fool. That foolish feeling escalated when my boyfriend wanted to go to the skating rink to hang out with his friends knowing that at eight months pregnant I would not be able to go. My words to him were if you truly loved me you would not even want to go without me. He replied what does love have to do with it? Those words hurt me to the core of my heart. I think it hurt the baby's heart to because I felt my first contraction. At that moment, I don't know what was hurting worse the heart pains or the contractions. Once I arrived at the hospital, the doctor informed me that I was not in labor. I was having what they called Braxton Hicks contractions. However, the baby was in position and could come any day.

Messages from your Social Circle

Think about the messages and or advice received from the members of your social circles. List the name of each person and the advice in which they gave. After completing the chart complete the reflection questions listed on the next page.

1.	2.	3.	4.	5.

Reflection Questions

1. When you think about your pregnancy experience what was the most difficult part for you to understand or accept?

_____

_____

2. How did you feel?

_____

_____

3. What your thoughts?

_____

_____

4. What did you believe?

_____

_____

5. What did you learn?

_____

_____

Scene Two

Take a deep breath. You have done a lot of work. You have just completed reflecting and processing your pregnancy experience. Those of you who are currently pregnant may want to stop here and wait to continue after the birth of your baby or continue to the next section to get a sneak preview in preparation for the after birth festivities. Those of you who have given birth should sit back relax and press through to the next section as the earthquake happens and you are shifted into your new role as teenage mother.

When Two Worlds Collide

The doctors announce congratulations it's a boy or it's a girl and in a matter of minutes your life is forever changed. The collision happens and you are transformed from a teenager to a teen mother. The funny thing is you don't feel any different but everyone around you expects you to think differently. The people around you behave differently. The same people who were not supportive of you when you revealed that you were pregnant are the same people who are the first to come to see the baby. You look at this creature and think wow this was growing inside me. You sit back a watch as the members of your social circle act as though it is Christmas morning and you have a new toy. It is like you become invisible and nothing is important but this new toy.

All of the mothers that are in attendance feel the need to discuss their birthing experience. Each story get more dramatic with the number of hours they were in labor, the place in which they gave birth and lack of medication they received. It is like a motherhood initiation ritual. You sit and watch this scene play out and try to make sense of the racing thoughts going through your mind. You try to understand the mixed emotions you are experiencing about your new role as mother. What does it truly mean to be a mother? That is the question that continues to be in the back of your mind.

Rather or not the baby's father has decided to take part in the festivities also produces a level of stress and anxiety. If he is not there you may feel abandoned and alone. You wonder what you will tell the baby about its father. If the baby's father is present you may feel a serious strain in the relationship as you move from teenage a courtship to a parenting partnership.

Teen Parent Responses

Have you ever noticed that when you are pregnant that some family members don't want to be around you but when you give birth to the child they are seen very often around you? And the ones that are around you when you are pregnant, they help you inn all but they go straight to the baby. They don't even say hi to you, or better yet know that you are there. I find that weird and funny at the same time.

My Story

As irony would have it, the aunt that physically assaulted me when she found out I was pregnant was the same aunt that was in the delivery room when I gave birth to my son. My son's father was playing basketball that night and swears that it was the best game he ever played. After the game, the friends that introduced us brought him to the hospital to see the baby. He stayed the night at the hospital.

His parents arrived at the hospital the next day to see the baby. He took his parents to the nursery to see their grandson. His father declared that there was not a black baby in the nursery. All the way down the corridors of the hospital my son's father and his father continued to argue about him not being the father of my son. As a side note prior to me becoming pregnant most of my friends were white. One of my white male friends committed suicide during the time I was pregnant. There was a rumor going around that he could have been my son's father.

Well so much for the plan. So now my son's father is not speaking to his father and I am not speaking to my mother. The baby now has no home to go home to. We are in a crisis with really no place to turn. I did not even have any way to get home from the hospital. My son's father could not use his parents car and none of my immediate family members had a car at the time. My son's father borrowed his cousin's pick-up truck to pick me up from the hospital. The baby had to stay in the hospital for a few extra days due to having a disease called jaundice. That gave us some time to come up with a game plan.

I arrived at my grandmother's house in pain after riding in a pick-truck for an hour. Every hump and bump reminded that I had in fact given birth. My son's father and I explained the situation that occurred at the hospital concerning his parents and my grandmother agreed to allow the baby to come to her home temporarily once he was released from the hospital.

Christmas day came early in 1992. December 10, 2010 to be exact. The day that my son came home from the hospital. My entire family was at my grandmother's house once we arrived. My mother whom I had not spoken to in eight months was there. She had bought every gadget known to man for her newborn grandson. I set back in disbelief as this newborn baby was showered with all of this attention. I immediately felt invisible and even jealous of the attention the baby was receiving. I thought to myself wow. What is next on the horizon?

Reflection Questions

How did the relationship change with individuals in your social circle after informing them about the pregnancy?

_____

_____

Did your relationship change after the baby was born?

_____

_____

How did this experience affect you socially and/or emotionally?

_____

_____

Patience and Perseverance have a magical effect before which difficulties disappear and obstacles vanish.

John Quincy Adams

Learning on the Job

The four to six weeks that you are home after the birth of the baby quickly comes to an end. It is now time to face the world. You think to yourself how am I going to handle this juggling act of going to school and motherhood. The first task at hand is to determine who is going to care for the baby while you are in school. The second task is the coordination of the drop off and the pick- up and schedule. You are afraid to think about the multitude of tasks that you are faced with before even walking out the door. On a pray you make it through the first mourning of packing bottle pampers and change of clothes, getting yourself and the baby dressed, feeding the baby and getting you both to your destinations. You are totally exhausted by the time you get to school but you think to yourself "I did it" so just maybe I can do this all again tomorrow. On the way home you are faced with homework, papers, projects and a baby that requires your time and attention. So rather morning or evening the juggling act never ends. You must learn time management skills quickly and prioritizing your time. But where do you learn the necessary skills to function within your dysfunctional world. You are faced with the task of learning on the job through trial and error. Somehow you develop a system of what time to wake up, back the baby bag, what time to wake up the baby to get he or she fed and dressed, and find a way to look half decent to face the world all on a limited amount of sleep. This all works fine unless something happens to throw a monkey wench in your plan like a sick baby or a sick baby sitter. Now What????????????? You must come up with plan B and keep it moving.

To function in the dysfunction of being a teen mom developing the skills for prioritizing and time management are of the upmost importance. Take some time to complete the next two exercises on prioritizing and time management.

Take a week and write down all the things you do in a given day on each hour. Then look to see where your priorities are.

1. Look for ways to be more efficient with your time.

2. Are you spending more time on things that are not important like texting, talking on the phone, watching television as a way to escape the reality of your life?

3. How much time are you spending talking and reading to your baby?

4. Are you doing your homework or waiting to the last minute to throw something together just to say you turned something in?

5. How much time are you spending trying to track your child's father down or worrying about what he is or is not doing?

Once you complete the time management worksheet. Code each item with a number that reflects its priority level. If you find yourself spending too much time in things that are not high priorities, change your priorities. Focus on the items that will benefit you and your baby long term.

Code 1- Must be done now or consequences will result.
Example: Tending to the Babies Needs

Code 2- Important to my life dreams and goals.
Example: Completing school Assignments

Code 3- Seems urgent, but if I skip it nothing bad will happen.
Example: Baby Daddy Drama

Code 4- Not important, not urgent, time wasters.
Example: Watching TV

Time Management Chart

• List all your scheduled items in column one of a day and code the priority level of each activity.

TIME	Monday	Tuesday	Wednes-day	Thursday	Friday	Saturday	Sunday
7am							
8am							
9am							
10am							
11am							
Noon							
1pm							
2pm							
3pm							
4pm							
5pm							
6pm							
7pm							
8pm							
9pm							
10pm							
11pm							
12am							

My Story

All I can say is thank God for grandmothers. My grandmother agreed to allow the baby and I to live with her to the end of the school year. So we had about six months to come up with a new plan. My boyfriend's grandmother agreed to take care of the baby while we went to school. To ease the stress and the pressure of getting ready in the morning we divided up clothes pampers and supplies to leave at his grandmother's house and my grandmother's house. Fortunately, my boyfriend had a car and could pick the baby and I up drop off the baby with his grandmother and take us to school.

I walked around school with a cloud of gloom around me not really interacting with my peers. I was depressed but determined to successful despite what came my way. The end of the school year was coming to a close and decisions needed to be made about our next steps. My boyfriend was a senior and was trying to decide what his future outlook would be with the new role of fatherhood attached. My grandmother decided that I should move to Atlanta to live with my mother at the end of the school year. Her rationale was that she had raised her children and her grand children, she was not going to raise her great-grand child as well. So the decision was made. My son and I would up to move to Atlanta.

My boyfriend was still trying to decide on his options after high school. I will never forget being over to his parents' house when a recruiter came to sell him on the idea that the military was his best option. The recruiter was selling him on the fact that he would be able to go to college for free and still be able to take care of his family. My boyfriend's father was not very fond of the idea of his son going to the military because in his bad experience in the military. He had however wholeheartedly accepted our son as his grandson. His father's advice to him that day hurt me to the core of my soul. His father said son the military is not a place for you. You need to come up with another plan. I want you to always take care of your son but you don't need to marry her or go to the military to do that. Flash backs from the voices of my social circle flooded my mind. Where do I go from here?

The Tragedy In Life doesn't lie in not reaching your goal. The tragedy lives in not having a goal to reach.

Benjamin Mays

Where Do We Go From Here?

When you do not have a road map your create one. How do you create a road map when you have no idea of where you want to go. You know that you must go, but go where. You feel something inside you pushing and propelling you toward a certain direction, but you are fearful. Afraid to make the wrong step or another wrong decision, fear seems to paralyze you. You wish desperately for a GPS system that you could type in your goals and dreams and it spit back step by step directions on how to reach your destination. It could inform you of the road blocks and obstacles that come your way and provide you with a way of escape.

Then you soon realize that is not reality and making a decision to do something is better than not making a decision to do anything. The fear of the unknown slowly fades away with each act of faith and determined step. The path becomes clearer and a beacon of light begins to shine as you begin a path toward your destiny. You are excited about your new road map and want to share it with others. Only to find that they can't see the beacon of light that you see. You sit back and wonder maybe I did not see the light at all.

This becomes a pivotal point in your life. Making a decision to make something from nothing takes courage. You must defy the odds and stay focused on the light even when no one around you supports or believes that the light exists.

My Story

The school year came to an abrupt end. My boy friend walked across the stage with a 3.8 grade point average and no plan. I had a plan however, one that was developed for me. I would be shipped off to Atlanta to live with my mother at sixteen years old with a baby, a disaster waiting to happen. My mother was convinced that the harder she could make life for me the better. Upon my arrival to Atlanta the first order of business was for me to get a job. My step father gave me my first job. I begin working on my sixteenth birthday at a Church's Chicken down town across from Spelman, Morehouse, Clark, and Morris Brown.

By some strange luck, my boyfriend decided to move to Atlanta with a cousin work for a year and then began college. I was enrolled in an open campus high school in College Park. The school had a daycare center attached to it. The school was designed for student to work at their own pace to complete their graduation requirements. In the new student orientation the Principal spoke words of inspiration and hope. He stated that a student could enter the school without any credits, be focused and could complete all their graduation requirements in two years. I began to get excited because I was an eleventh grader. I started to make plans in my mind to complete two years worth of work in one year.

The school counselors gave out the transcript evaluations that listed all the courses that were needed for graduation. I began goal setting that day. I outlined my plan of action. I determined how long I could spend in each course in order to reach my goal of graduating by the end of the year. There is nothing better than to set a goal and reach it. I began to see some success in my plan. I only had one obstacle, we could not take the text books home. I began to sneak the text books out of the classroom so I could stay up at night and on the weekends to get ahead. Instead of reading my son nursery rhymes and children books, I read him World History, American Literature, and Biology. I told him that he was going to be the smartest baby on the planet because he and I was a team and I needed his help to pass the classes.

I learned a very important lesson during this time about sharing your goals and dreams. I walked inside the school counselor's office having completed another set of courses one Friday and informed her of my plan to complete high school a year early. She informed me not to get my hopes up, that it had never been done before but to keep up the good work I was doing. It was like my eyes had been opened to the harsh reality of my life. Prior to that moment my focus on the goal protected me from the reality of my situation. I did not think about having to walk to the train station rather rain, sleet or snow to catch the train across town to hand the baby over to his father, get back on the train travel down town to work, get off work, get home stay up doing homework and surviving off of four hours of sleep per day. I began to self sabotage.

My boyfriend was off of work on Mondays and Tuesdays. So the next Monday, instead of going to school I went over to his apartment and spent the day with him. We had a wonderful day of playing house that Monday so I thought that it would be a great idea to so again the next day. However the next day was different, I arrived to his apartment and he would not open the door. Speaking to me through the chain on the door he spoke words that cut through to my soul. His words were what are you doing here? Why are you not at school? I don't want a dummy. I got my high school diploma now you need to get yours. There is nothing like a reality check to propel you into your destiny. From that moment forward, I never let anything or anyone keep me from attending school.

I went to school no matter what. I would even take the baby to school sick. Thank heavens for Mrs. Harriet Shell in the daycare center at the school that made sure that my son was taken care of and would direct me on what to do and when he had an ear infection, diarrhea, fever, teething, because I was at a loss. I did reach my goal and I graduated my junior year of high school. The day I graduated I moved in with my boyfriend and began to play house but soon learned that life was not a game.

Understand that obstacles are just a part of the game.
Whatever you can imagine you can achieve.

Russell Simmons

Scene Three

Getting the Needs Met

Welcome to the adult world. You are now in the position to leave the negative events from the past behind and design a new script for your life. The main focus of this new scene is the day to day needs of caring for yourself and your child. Clear vision is needed during this. You must open yourself up to find the necessary fortitude to accomplish the task at hand. You must look inside to find the passion needed to survive and provide the love necessary to care for your child emotionally even when you don't feel like it. You must look behind to evaluate the lessons learned so you will not repeat the same mistakes. You must look around to evaluate the resources available to you that will enable you to provide for your child's physical needs. You must look up to obtain spiritual guidance to withstand all of the challenges that will come your way. Open your eyes, your heart and your mind and embrace your new role because mommies make things happen.

My Story

My boyfriend and I developed a master plan on how we could both go to college and work and take care of our son. His parents agreed to take care of our son for the first semester so we could get things in order. He and I both were trying to go to work and school with one car. This presented great challenges because my college was not on the bus line. The first order of business was for me to get a car. My mom had three cars in her drive way but would not let me use one of them. So I ventured off to the car dealership and purchased my first car without a driver's license with the help of my step father.

The decision was made that I would attend Clayton State College. I was able to obtain enough financial aid to cover all of the expenses for attending college. However, daily I would have to face the fact that I would be serving chicken to the students attended Spelman and I would not be able to attend.

The time came for my orientation for college. I spoke with my advisor and informed her that I wanted to major in psychology. She informed me that a Bachelors in Psychology would not be a good idea because it would not pay enough money. Her words were you would make about the same amount of money as a job at McDonalds would pay. So I suggest that you major in something else for your Bachelors and then pursue a Masters in Psychology. I left the advisor office lost with a book of majors in hand. After much thought I decided to just get a certification in Medical Assisting which would take one year so I could at least get a better job than I was currently working.

I began to work the plan, our son came home and was placed in a daycare with another family member child just in case an emergency would come up someone else could pick him up. I went to college on Mondays, Wednesdays, and Fridays and my boyfriend went on Tuesdays and Thursdays. We were able to maintain our daily needs. I completed my program and obtained a job working at an Ear, Nose, and Throat Practice. We even took our first family vacation to Tennessee. The needs were getting met but I was not satisfied with my life. Struggling to make ends meet was not the life I wanted to live. I was very unhappy and thought the problem was we were not married. A name change will fix everything.

"I don't think of myself as a poor deprived ghetto girl you made good. I think of myself as somebody, who from an early age, knew I was responsible for myself and I had to make good."

Oprah Winfrey

Who am I

What's in a name? The name that I had been given "Baby Mama" hunted me like a ghost in a haunted house. No matter what level of success I achieved it really didn't matter much because in my mind I was still a statistic and someone's baby mama. I lived my life in a state of fear that I would fulfill the prophecy present by my infamous social circle. I fought hard to reveal my true identity but how could I expect others to see what I could not see.

Please look at me and see that I am more than my situation and bigger than my circumstances was my daily plea. Who am I? I would endure a long painful road of self discovery, self love, and self acceptance to bring closure to the wounds created by the words "BABY MAMA".

My Story

On Christmas morning the burning question that plagued my mine became the topic of conversation. As we watch our son open his presents under the tree I asked so do you plan on marrying me. His response was we are not in a position to be thinking about getting married. When I get married I am going to bring my wife home to a house and not to an apartment.

A house that is it. I began to develop a plan. House, Name Change, Bachelors degree then I would be happy. I begin searching to find out everything about what was needed to buy a house. My mother was the only person I knew that owned a home and I was not going to ask her. I was lost. As luck would have it a patient came into the doctor's office that was a real estate agent. I spoke with her about my desire to purchase a home. I was nineteen and my boyfriend was twenty-one at the time. She told me everything I would need and I began collecting the necessary documents and about five months later we had purchased our first home.

Our parents were very shocked, surprised, and not very supportive. My mom said you won't have it long. His father said son you just signed your life away for a house for that girl. So the joy of the home purchase was quickly dimmed by the messages from the infamous social circle.

Now with a mortgage, two car notes, daycare, and college the stress level increased dramatically. Many times I would not have a baby sister to watch my son while I attended class. I would take my son to class with me. I would have long talks to him about what mommy needed him to do and he would sit in class and color being a quiet as he could be so he could help his mommy.

The relationship between my boyfriend and I was like a dormant volcano waiting to erupt. Neither one of was saying anything but the tension in the air was extremely think. That volcano finally erupted with the announcement that I was pregnant again. Our son was four years old at the time almost done with daycare and ready to begin regular school, which would have reduced our expenses. The light at the end of the tunnel quickly faded with the announcement of the pending new arrival to the family. The additional stress added pressure to an already overloaded system.

My life became like a re-run on steroids. My pregnancy this time was considered a high risk. I had to stop working and going school at three months and be placed on bed rest. At this time the volcano is erupting daily because of the stress to maintain all of the financial responsibility, the care of our son and ultimately the care of me. The doctor's order was that I was only supposed to get out of bed to go the bathroom and back to bed in fear that I would lose the baby.

My boyfriend would claim that he was working over time, double shifts or any excuse just to not have to come home and deal with the realty that face him there. I cried for breakfast, lunch and dinner. He was out living his life and I was trapped in the house trying to hold on to baby number two.

Things went from bad to worse. I was placed in the hospital at six months because I went into labor. The doctors were able to stop the labor but I would have to remain in the hospital until the baby was born. That would be for six weeks. For six weeks I was hooked up to IV's, monitored around the clock, and told the negative repercussions of having a pre-mature baby. I was reminded that if they could not hold me from having the baby until a certain point that my baby may die, her brain or lungs may not fully develop, and that she may have learning difficulties.

I even missed my son's first day at kindergarten. I was angry, depressed, and very confused. I had a home, a pretty ok job, I was in college working on my degree, but I was not happy. I had accomplished things at twenty years old that no one in my family had ever done, but the messages from the infamous social circle begin to flood my mind and inform me of who and what I was. I was a sperm receptacle, a baby mama, and now I am on baby number two for a man that is going to fill me up with a house full of kids and leave me. Oh yes! You know that men can't be trusted and will always let you down.

I remember giving birth to my daughter at seven and a half months with her father holding my hand I prayed that my daughter would not die and clarity to make a decision about where I would go home to after leaving the hospital. I needed a plan. But a plan would have to wait because the baby was only 3lbs and would have to stay in the hospital a couple of weeks prior to coming home.

Changing Your Mind

We are all born with the potential for both straight and crooked thinking. We can choose to focus and direct our thoughts toward a path of happiness, love and growth or allow our faulty thinking to take us on a winding road to intolerance, perfectionism, blaming and avoidance of our actual growth potential.

We often sabotage our movement toward growth because of our inborn tendency toward distorted thinking and self-defeating patterns. We have developed a set of rules or expectations for how we ourselves and others should behave. Our level or happiness or satisfaction with ourselves and others decreases when these self imposed standards are not achieved.

We make a huge mistake when we make our personal preferences for love, approval, and success dire needs. We expect other people to change to suit our preference. We believe if we add enough pressure or passion to the situation we can effect change. We practice self-denial and sacrifice our selves greatly for what we perceive as dire needs to be fulfilled. When we don't receive the desired reward we become bitter and resentful.

We transfer the responsibility for our pain and pleasure to other people. We give them the ultimate power over making or breaking our day. We compare ourselves to others trying to determine who is smarter or more attractive and the mere thought of not measuring up alters our emotional state.

We must take ownership and responsibility for creating our own happiness. I challenge you to change your mind from the outside in. Change your mind by changing your language. Use self-talks to guide your thoughts. Evaluate your thoughts and reactions to the situations, people and events in your life and make a decision to walk in love, peace and happiness. Remember your A B C's. The activating thought (A) does not cause the (C) the emotional consequence; instead (B) your personal thoughts and beliefs about (A) cause (C) the emotional reaction.

When you change playgrounds you must change play mates.

Mayor Kasim Reed

Developing Your Circle of Influence

When you are in a delicate emotional state it is very important that you monitor what you allow into your inner circle. At this critical time you must monitor what you see, hear and even speak. Your words have power to speak death or speak life to your situation. Change is the main order of business. You must change your mind and monitor your thought. Change the people in your life and replace your social circle with a circle of influence.

The same people that were able to provide guidance for you to get to this point in your life may not be able to guide you to your next phase in life. The same friends that were at one phase of life with you may not be ready to move to the next phase. This may be an uncomfortable feeling as shed the skin of your former life to renew and develop the life that you always dreamed of.

This purging must occur or you will remain stagnate or worse go backward. Think about people in mathematical terms. Some people come into your life and add (+) value. They in some way make your life better. Some people come into your life and multiply (x) you or propel you into a new direction you did not even know was possible. In the alternative some people come into your life and subtract (-) from you through their negativity always taking and never giving back. At worse some people divide (/) you. Reduce you down to someone you don't even recognize anymore. This usually occurs through mental and physical abuse.

Seek out people that are going in the direction you are going in.

Don't be afraid to ask for professional help. Your mental health is just as important as your physical health. So let's begin developing the life you want by removing the items that subtract and reduce your chances of reaching your full potential.

Reflection Activity

Think about the ten closest people to you or the ten people you spend the most time with. List them in and identify the mathematical sign (+, -, x, /) that represents the purpose they play in your life and why. The people that are not adding or assisting you to reach your goals maybe people you may want to consider limiting your contact and communication.

Individuals Names	Mathematical Sign	Rational
1.		
2.		
3.		
4.		
5.		
6.		
7.		
8.		
9.		
10.		

Identify each person that was given a subtraction sign or a division sign and work through the following exercise.

1. I am feeling or felt_____ by _____.

2. I feel this way because_____.

3. What I expected was _____.

4. When I realized what I expected was not what I was receiving I _____.

5. I believe that as a result of this experience I _____
   _____

6. This experience has taught me _____.

7. I am ready and willing to release all the negative, thoughts, feeling and beliefs related to _____.

8. I am choosing to release _____ from my inner circle.

When you work hard, your dreams do come true. But what do you do when life exceeds your dreams? You dream bigger. If people don't laugh at you when you share your dream, then you are not dreaming big enough. Make them Laugh Dream Big.

Travis Smiley

My Story

Unless you create the vision you want for your life you will quickly follow what and who ever is willing to lead. You will never be satisfied living your life to fulfill other people's expectation of you. In my case I was so consumed with not being what my social circle said I was going to be that I could not be the person that I truly wanted to be. I spent many years trying to build a life that would suit the nay sayers and never once did I ask the question what I wanted my life to look like. I was so consumed with what other people would say or think that I was headed for self-destruction.

The first thing I did was decide that no material possession was worth my sanity so I moved from my home back in with my mother for six months. Ironically this occurred on Mother's Day. This was a very hard pill to swallow but I needed to find myself I felt that I needed to take a step back in order to take a step forward.

I worked three jobs during this time to save money. I was determined that my children and I would be in our own place by Thanksgiving. We moved into an apartment the beginning of November. I would never forget setting up the Christmas tree after Thanksgiving Dinner in my first apartment. The children and I turned on the Christmas music and danced around the room placing the ornaments on the tree without rhyme or reason into the wee hours of the mourning. That night and many nights that followed I cried. But these tears were purging tears. These were tears washing away the fear and doubt. These tears were fertilizing the seeds of my dreams and goals.

I learned a great lesson during this time. You can't hold on and move on at the same time. Even though I had moved on, I wanted to control what my boyfriend was doing all in the name of concern for the children. This was a great challenge for me. I sought help from a mental health professional to undo the negative thinking patterns that I was using as arsenals to destroy my life.

With the move into the apartment, I did not have a lot of money for Christmas presents. I talked to my babies about the real meaning of Christmas and dispelled the myth about Santa Clause. We decided that they would receive three small items as a token of celebration of the season to reenact the three items Jesus received from the wise men. This became our little family tradition.

I was always open and honest with my children about our financial situation and we would have discussions on the choices or sacrifices we would need to make in order to make ends meet. My son became my human calculator making sure that we always stayed within budget. He was always concerned about his mommy. I would sometimes take them out to eat to celebrate a good week in school or success on a test. On one of these trips I did not order anything to eat for myself. My son said mommy I am not that hungry you can have half of my hamburger. I reassured him that I was fine and did not need to eat his food. I learned that my children were very in tune with my emotions. So no matter how bleak the situation seemed I would always find a way to see a positive. The power of positive thinking really works!

You can't have the life you want until you know what it looks like. Just as a builder requires a blueprint to build a house you need a blue print to build your life. Take the time to process what your ideal life would include and then start building.

1. Describe your currently life as it relates to your family, friends, job, financial and health.

2. How do you feel about your current situation?

3. What does your ideal life look like?

4. Who are the individuals that are apart of this new life?

5. How do you feel in the new life?

6. How can you begin to create this new life?

7. What will be your first step in designing your new life?

My Story

The New Year sparked a rebirth or renewal of my perspective about life. I created a vision for my life and began to dream again. I begin setting goals and making plans. I developed a vision book listing all the things I wanted to accomplish in life. Best of all I begin to enjoy the process of reaching the milestones I set for myself. I began to expect success and developed a winning mentality. I filled my life with positive people and removed negativity from my life no matter what the source.

The first goal I reached five months into the New Year. On New Year's Eve I wished that my children and I could have a home again. One day we were dream casting and drove through this new subdivision that was being built. Not even thinking about purchasing a home at the time, we got out to look at the model homes. Upon giving the agent my information within a few moments he returned and said the mortgage company thinks they can get you approved so pick out the floor plan you like. I was able to purchase my second home. I was twenty two at this time. Being able to walk into my own 4 bedroom 3 bathroom home with two children was one of the proudest days of my life.

My next focus was on my education. I went out and bought empty degree frames and put them on the wall. Daily I would pass the wall and say that one day that the frames would be filled with a bachelors, masters and doctorate degrees. I ended up with seven degrees when it was all said and done

I got my children involved in the dream. They knew all about my goals and dreams. Another one of my dreams was to drive a Mercedes CLK. My children and I would drive down the road and yell out that's mommy's car every time we would see the model. Several years later I was able to reach that goal and all of the goals that were listed prior.

I was determined for my children to know that dreams do come true. At eight years old my son had a dream of going on a boat for his birthday. He and I discussed the cost of going on the boat and we agreed that we would go on the boat instead of buying Christmas presents. We celebrated his birthday on a cruise to the Bahamas that year. It was my first time going outside of the country. I made a vow that I would make sure that it would not be our last. Seeing the world became a goal. We listed all the places we wanted to visit and each year we were able to check them off annually as a goal achieved.

My daughter's dream was to go to Disney World to Cinderella's castle. There is nothing more powerful than to stand and watch the fireworks show at Disney World and listen to the Disney song *When you wish upon a star all your dreams will come true.* The only thing better is to hear your baby say "Mommy my dream came true. I am at Disney World standing in front of Cinderella's Castle." I shed a different kind of tears that day, tears of joy.

So now start dreaming. Your baby is counting on you to live your life to your greatest potential. Create a vision, develop a plan of action and get to WORK.

Lessons for Growth

1. Examine yourself on a regular basis. If you are not willing to examine yourself and grow you are bound to repeat the same cycle of mistakes.

2. Re-evaluate your friendships on a regular basis. If these relationships are not adding value to your life consider limiting your contact or communication with these individuals.

3. Clearly identify and communicate your expectations to yourself and others.

4. Ask for exactly what you want.

5. Be open to everything but attached to nothing.

6. Accept responsibility for everything you do and experience.

7. Choose to see situations as life lessons instead of disappointment.

8. Seek God the giver of wisdom, knowledge and direction.

9. Encourage yourself. Be your biggest cheerleader. Develop a winning mentality.

About The Author

Dr. Lateshia Woodley is a Counseling Psychologist and Educational Consultant that specializes in transformation initiatives and change management. She is a licensed professional counselor, a nationally certified counselor and certified school counselor. The founder of Dynamic Achievement Solutions, LLC

Dr. Woodley .provides counseling services in the following areas: individual therapy, trauma, and major life transitions for adolescents and adults. She lectures and provides teen parenting workshops, with the mission to ignite, motivate and encourage individuals to reach their full potential.

CPSIA information can be obtained at www.ICGtesting.com
225029LV00005B/162/P